MARY EMMERLING'S
American Country Christmas List Book

Photographs by Joshua Greene

Clarkson Potter/Publishers
New York

Published by Clarkson N. Potter, Inc., 201 East 50th Street, New York, New York 10022. Member of the Crown Publishing Group.

CLARKSON POTTER, POTTER, and colophon are trademarks of Clarkson N. Potter, Inc.

Manufactured in Hong Kong

Design by Renato Stanisic

ISBN 0-517-58870-6

10   9   8   7   6   5   4   3   2   1

First Edition

To Samantha and Jonathan, who make every Christmas a joy.
Peace and Joy to the World.

With special thanks to Jimmie Cramer and Dean
Johnson (I couldn't do these books without their wonderful
collections), Lester and Barbara Breininger
(who love Christmas in every room of the house), Eliza Rand,
Bobbie Sanchez, and, as always, to Joshua Greene.

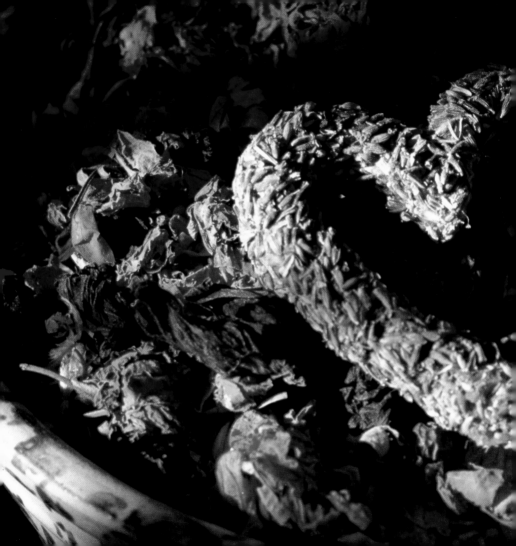

CONTENTS

INTRODUCTION

I *survive by making lists all year round, but never more than during the Christmas holidays. Christmas comes on the same day every year, but somehow it seems to sneak up on us suddenly and slip away unless we get well organized in advance. Since my two children, Samantha and Jonathan, both have their birthdays in December, the Christmas season at our house is always a little livelier — and busier. I find that if I am really well prepared, I enjoy the festivities a lot more, and so does everyone else. I have always wanted a holiday notebook like this one that would help me make my lists and keep them all in one place, ready to* be tucked away and consulted next year when it's time to buy the presents and mail the cards. It is also intended as a keepsake book, for recording notes about recipes and decorating and for preserving a swatch of gift wrap or a photograph of your family gathered around the tree. For your holiday organizing and your holiday memories, I hope my American Country Christmas List Book works as well for you as it has for me.

Mary Emmerling

CHRISTMAS
CARDS

T he tradition of sending Christmas cards is just a century old, but it seems like it must have been part of the holidays forever. Whatever kind of Christmas card you like to send — from handmade to store-bought, a photograph of your family or a card from your favorite charity — it is a wonderful way to keep up your network of friends and to let them know, at least once a year, that you are thinking of them.

The Christmas cards you receive are instant holiday decorations (and of course the more cards you send, the more you are likely to receive). You can tuck them in an antique latticework rack, or line them up with greens on the mantel, or toss them in an old basket next to your easy chair, where you can read and reread the notes from your friends. Use these pages to record your Christmas cards; you will know where to find the list for next year, and you won't have to make messy notations in your address book.

Name	YEAR _____		YEAR _____	
	Card Sent	Card Received	Card Sent	Card Received

Name	YEAR ____		YEAR ____	
	Card Sent	Card Received	Card Sent	Card Received

Name	YEAR _____		YEAR _____	
	Card Sent	Card Received	Card Sent	Card Received

Name	YEAR _____		YEAR _____	
	Card Sent	Card Received	Card Sent	Card Received

Name	YEAR_____		YEAR_____	
	Card Sent	*Card Received*	*Card Sent*	*Card Received*
_____	_____	_____	_____	_____
_____	_____	_____	_____	_____
_____	_____	_____	_____	_____
_____	_____	_____	_____	_____
_____	_____	_____	_____	_____
_____	_____	_____	_____	_____
_____	_____	_____	_____	_____
_____	_____	_____	_____	_____
_____	_____	_____	_____	_____
_____	_____	_____	_____	_____
_____	_____	_____	_____	_____
_____	_____	_____	_____	_____
_____	_____	_____	_____	_____
_____	_____	_____	_____	_____
_____	_____	_____	_____	_____
_____	_____	_____	_____	_____
_____	_____	_____	_____	_____
_____	_____	_____	_____	_____
_____	_____	_____	_____	_____
_____	_____	_____	_____	_____
_____	_____	_____	_____	_____
_____	_____	_____	_____	_____

| Name | YEAR _____ | | YEAR _____ | |
	Card Sent	Card Received	Card Sent	Card Received

Name	YEAR _____		YEAR _____	
	Card Sent	*Card Received*	*Card Sent*	*Card Received*

Christmas Presents

No matter how many people I have on my present list each Christmas, I like to look back and see just who gave whom what in years past. This is not so much in order to match the gifts I give to the gifts I receive, but so I don't duplicate last year's present to a family member or friend. What others give me is a good indication of what they like, too.

You can also use the list to track gifts as you buy them, as I do, throughout the year. Then you won't forget that handmade basket for Aunt Lucy you picked up on vacation in Maine last summer and stowed in the back of a closet. And if you are budgeting your Christmas allowance, you can make note of your expenditures along the way.

When the holiday has passed and the tree has been taken down, it's time to dash off those thank-you notes (I still try to get mine out before New Year's Day) — and check them off as you mail them.

FAMILY

YEAR _____

Name	Gave	Received	Thanks Sent
_____	_____	_____	{ }
_____	_____	_____	{ }
_____	_____	_____	{ }
_____	_____	_____	{ }
_____	_____	_____	{ }
_____	_____	_____	{ }
_____	_____	_____	{ }
_____	_____	_____	{ }
_____	_____	_____	{ }
_____	_____	_____	{ }
_____	_____	_____	{ }
_____	_____	_____	{ }
_____	_____	_____	{ }
_____	_____	_____	{ }
_____	_____	_____	{ }
_____	_____	_____	{ }

FAMILY

YEAR _____

Name	Gave	Received	Thanks Sent
			{ }
			{ }
			{ }
			{ }
			{ }
			{ }
			{ }
			{ }
			{ }
			{ }
			{ }
			{ }
			{ }
			{ }
			{ }
			{ }
			{ }

FAMILY

YEAR _____

Name	Gave	Received	Thanks Sent
			{ }
			{ }
			{ }
			{ }
			{ }
			{ }
			{ }
			{ }
			{ }
			{ }
			{ }
			{ }
			{ }
			{ }
			{ }
			{ }

FRIENDS

YEAR _____

Name	Gave	Received	Thanks Sent
			{ }
			{ }
			{ }
			{ }
			{ }
			{ }
			{ }
			{ }
			{ }
			{ }
			{ }
			{ }
			{ }
			{ }
			{ }
			{ }

FRIENDS

YEAR _____

Name	Gave	Received	Thanks Sent
_____	_____	_____	{ }
_____	_____	_____	{ }
_____	_____	_____	{ }
_____	_____	_____	{ }
_____	_____	_____	{ }
_____	_____	_____	{ }
_____	_____	_____	{ }
_____	_____	_____	{ }
_____	_____	_____	{ }
_____	_____	_____	{ }
_____	_____	_____	{ }
_____	_____	_____	{ }
_____	_____	_____	{ }
_____	_____	_____	{ }
_____	_____	_____	{ }
_____	_____	_____	{ }

GRATUITIES AND BUSINESS GIFTS

Name	*Gave*	*Name*	*Gave*

HOLIDAY
ENTERTAINING

As readers of my books have no doubt realized, I always make a point of entertaining over the holidays. I love to decorate the house, set a mood, and show off the tree and trimmings to all of my friends. With candles in every room and the scent of pine boughs and spiced cider in the air, my home becomes a completely different place — a fantasyland that seems to make everyone happy.

This is no time to buck tradition, though you can certainly be creative in your menu planning. But you will probably want to serve some of the favorites again and again over the years, and recording them in this diary is one way to remember just exactly which recipes were special hits. You may elect to have several holiday occasions — a cocktail party for friends, a family dinner, a Christmas-morning breakfast, and even a special party just for the children. But never plan to do more than you really want to do. It should be a season for enjoying yourself as well as for pleasing others.

A HOLIDAY
CELEBRATION

DATE HELD _____

Guest List

_____ _____ _____

_____ _____ _____

_____ _____ _____

_____ _____ _____

_____ _____ _____

_____ _____ _____

_____ _____ _____

The Menu

_____

_____ _____ _____

_____ _____

_____

CHECKLIST

Invitations Mailed	{ }	*Ice*	{ }
Food Ordered	{ }	*Glasses*	{ }
Flowers	{ }	*Linens*	{ }
Decorations	{ }	*Coatrack*	{ }
Wine and Liquor	{ }	*Miscellaneous*	{ }

Notes for Next Year

_____

_____

_____

_____

_____

_____

_____

_____

_____

_____

_____

A HOLIDAY
CELEBRATION

DATE HELD _____

Guest List

_____ _____ _____

_____ _____ _____

_____ _____ _____

_____ _____ _____

_____ _____ _____

_____ _____ _____

_____ _____ _____

The Menu

_____

_____ _____ _____

_____ _____

_____

CHECKLIST

Invitations Mailed { }   Ice { }
Food Ordered { }   Glasses { }
Flowers { }   Linens { }
Decorations { }   Coatrack { }
Wine and Liquor { }   Miscellaneous { }

Notes for Next Year

_____

_____

_____

_____

_____

_____

_____

_____

_____

_____

_____

_____

HOLIDAY
DECORATING

What a wonderful excuse the Christmas season is to transform your home with evergreens, topiaries decorated like tiny trees, potted bulbs, treasured ornaments, colorful stockings and quilts, and candles large and small. I try not to go overboard, but I still like to do a lot — from the front door to the kitchen cabinets, my house lets you know it's a holiday.

Use this page to keep track of the decorations you store and bring out every year — and to make note of new ideas for next year. Remember to mark the boxes of decorations and stow them all in the same spot in the basement, closet, or attic. Bright-colored labels on the sides of boxes will help you locate them quickly when the time comes — and who wants to keep the family waiting around the naked tree? To prevent last-minute crises next Christmas Eve, purchase (at post-holiday sales) and pack away new trimmings, bulbs, and extension cords after the holiday this year.

Tree Trimmings

_____
_____
_____
_____
_____
_____
_____

Around the House

_____
_____
_____
_____
_____
_____
_____
_____
_____

Outdoors

_____
_____
_____
_____
_____
_____
_____
_____